Volcanoes

Christopher Durbin

HODDER
Wayland

an imprint of Hodder Children's Books

Geography First

Titles in this series

Coasts • Islands • Maps and Symbols
Mountains • Rivers • Volcanoes

© 2004 White-Thomson Publishing Ltd

Produced for Hodder Wayland by
White-Thomson Publishing Ltd
2/3 St Andrew's Place
Lewes, East Sussex
BN7 1UP

Geography consultant: John Lace, School Adviser
Editor: Katie Orchard
Picture research: Glass Onion Pictures
Designer: Chris Halls at Mind's Eye Design Ltd, Lewes
Artist: Peter Bull

Published in Great Britain in 2004 by Hodder Wayland,
an imprint of Hodder Children's Books.

The right of Christopher Durbin to be identified as the
author has been asserted by him in accordance with
the Copyright, Designs and Patents Act, 1988.

British Library Cataloguing in Publication Data
   Durbin, Christopher
   Volcanoes. – (Geography First)
   1. Volcanoes - Juvenile literature
   I. Title II. Orchard, Katie
   551.2'1
ISBN 0 7502 4355 4

Printed in China

Hodder Children's Books
A division of Hodder Headline Limited
338 Euston Road, London NW1 3BH

Cover: A volcanic eruption on the Galapagos islands.
Title page: A volcano smokes above the city of
Sakurajima, Japan.
Further information page: A man walks across the
smouldering Soufrière Volcano in St Lucia.

Acknowledgements:
The author and publisher would like to thank the following for their permission to reproduce the
following photographs: Eye Ubiquitous 24 (James Davis Travel Photography); Geoscience 5 (Hawaii Volcanoes
National Park/Bob Siebert), 9 (Professor S. Self), 11 (Solarfilma), 14 (Hawaii Volcanoes National Park), 18
(Hawaii Volcanoes National Park), 26 (Professor B. Booth); Frank Lane Picture Agency *cover*; Hodder Wayland
Picture Library *title page, chapter openers*, 13 (Associated Press), 31; Oxford Scientific Films 15 (Doug Allan),
17 (Konrad Wothe), 20 (Christian Grzimek/Okapia), 21 (T.C. Middleton), 23 (Tom Ulrich), 25 (David Tipling),
28; Popperfoto 7 (Richart Bouhet/Reuters), 16 (Romeo Ranoco/Reuters), 19 (Jacky Naegelen/Reuters), 27
(Reuters); Still Pictures 10 (Dominique Reymond/UNEP), 22 (Jeff and Alexa Henry).

Words in bold **like this** are explained in the glossary on page 30.

Contents

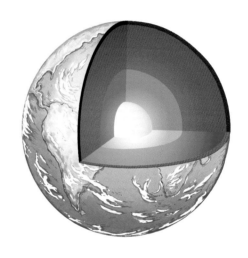

What is a volcano?

A volcano is a place where hot, liquid or **molten** rocks from deep underground are pushed up through a weak area in the Earth's surface.

The Earth is made up of layers. The centre is called the **core** and it is extremely hot. Surrounding the core is the **mantle**. This layer is made up of hot, molten, moving rock, called **magma**. The mantle is covered with a thin layer of rocks called the Earth's **crust**.

Layers of the Earth

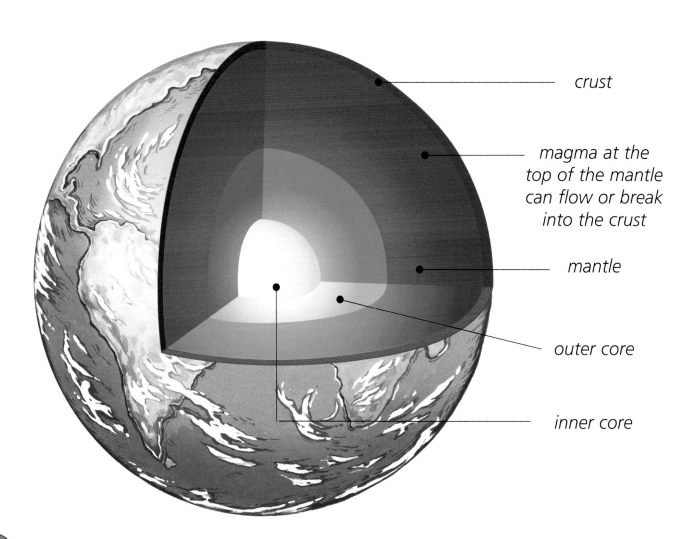

crust

magma at the top of the mantle can flow or break into the crust

mantle

outer core

inner core

Where the Earth's crust is cracked or thin, magma flows up, or **erupts**, to the surface, forming a volcano.

▼ *This scientist is studying Mauna Loa volcano, Hawaii, as it erupts.*

A fiery mountain

When magma erupts from the ground, it is called **lava**.
Lava is very hot – much, much hotter than boiling water.

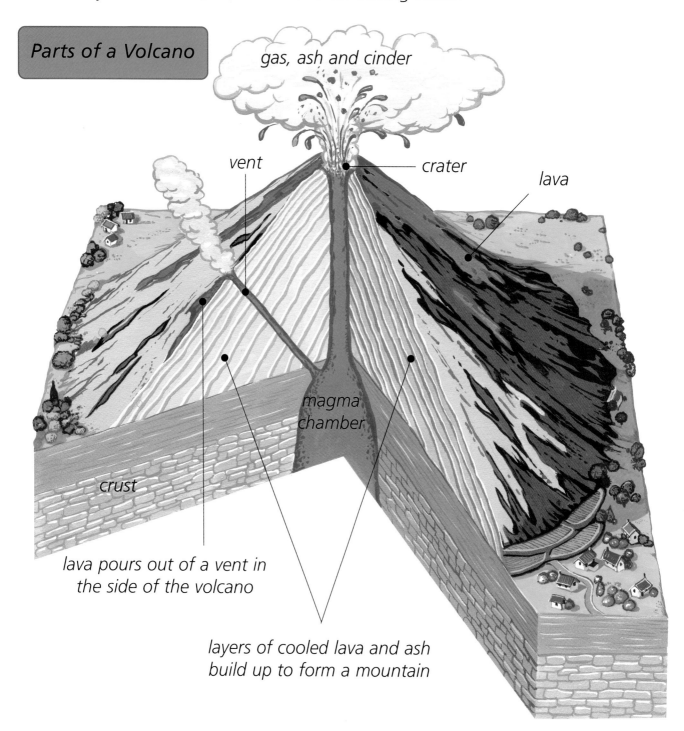

Parts of a Volcano

gas, ash and cinder

vent

crater

lava

magma chamber

crust

lava pours out of a vent in the side of the volcano

layers of cooled lava and ash build up to form a mountain

Gradually the lava cools down and becomes solid rock. Over time, as more lava flows out of the ground and cools down, it builds up to form a mountain.

Volcanoes are usually mountains with a bowl in the top, called a **crater**. Most eruptions happen in the crater. Sometimes lava flows through **chambers** or **vents** at the side of a volcano.

▲ *Onlookers stand by as this volcano in the Reunion Islands erupts in a fountain of fiery lava.*

The Earth's crust is like a cracked eggshell, made up of huge pieces called **plates**. Most volcanoes are found along the edges of plates, where the crust is cracked or thin. The plates are shown on the map on page 29.

The Earth's plates move slowly over time. Where the plates move apart, magma flows up between them, forming volcanoes.

When Plates Move

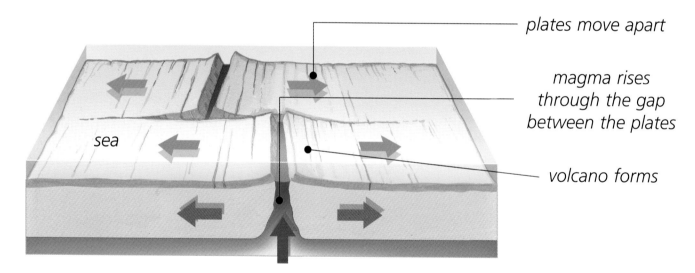

plates move apart

magma rises through the gap between the plates

volcano forms

sea

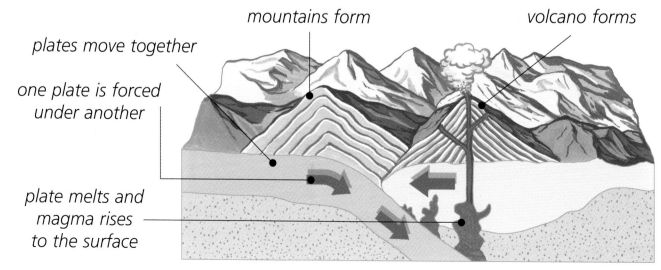

mountains form

volcano forms

plates move together

one plate is forced under another

plate melts and magma rises to the surface

In other places, plates collide, or crash into each other. One plate may slide under the other, forcing the crust to fold in on itself and form mountains. Gases and magma may push up to the surface through the crust here, too.

▼ *Ngauruhoe, in New Zealand, is part of a huge band of volcanoes around the Pacific Ocean called the 'Ring of Fire'.*

Undersea volcanoes

Volcanoes are not only found on land. At the bottom of some oceans, the plates of the Earth's crust move apart and lava erupts. Over time, layers of cooled lava gradually build up to create a long line of volcanoes under the sea.

▼ *When lava erupts into water it cools very quickly.*

Sometimes an undersea volcano erupts over and over again, gradually growing taller. Eventually the volcano may become so tall that it breaks through the surface of the sea to form an island.

▲ *Steam and ash erupt from Surtsey, a very young volcanic island near Iceland. It first rose out of the sea in the 1970s.*

Volcanic eruptions

Volcanoes do not all erupt in the same way. Some erupt constantly, producing runny lava that flows gently from the crater and sides. Others have frequent eruptions that explode like glowing fountains.

Some volcanoes explode unexpectedly, blasting a column of steam, gases, dust and **cinder**, small pieces of rock, high into the air.

constant eruption

long, runny lava flows

cinder and ash fall close to volcano

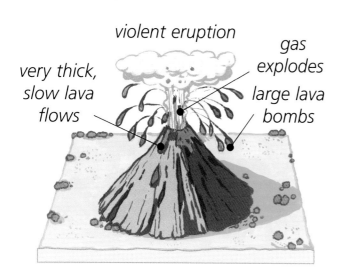

mild, regular eruptions

short, sticky lava flows

cinder and ash explode often

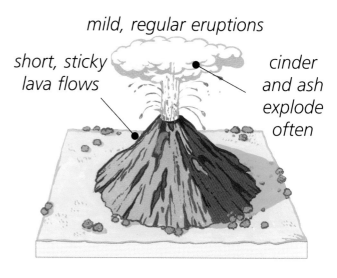

violent eruption

very thick, slow lava flows

gas explodes

large lava bombs

very large, explosive eruption

no lava flows

cinder and gas blasted into the air

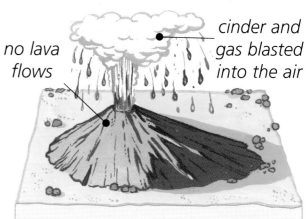

When a volcano erupts violently, ash, poisonous gas, cinder and rocks may flow rapidly down its slopes. This is called a **pyroclastic flow**.

▼ *Pyroclastic flows can travel at over 100 kilometres per hour. This man is running for his life.*

Different shapes

The shape and size of a volcano depend on the type of eruption and the type of lava it produces.

Some volcanoes have gentle eruptions, with thin, runny lava. This type of lava has a Hawaiian name, **Pa hoe hoe**. It may flow a long way before it cools down. Over time, big, wide mountains with gently sloping sides form. These are called **shield volcanoes**.

▼ *Runny Pa hoe hoe lava flows like a river from Kilauea volcano, in Hawaii.*

Other volcanoes may have gentle eruptions of runny lava followed by explosive eruptions of thick, sticky lava. Slow, sticky lava is given the Hawaiian name, **A a**. This cools down quickly and builds up around the crater to form a steep-sided cone shape.

▲ *Most volcanoes are cone shaped, like Tungurahua, in Ecuador.*

Destructive volcanoes

Volcanic eruptions can cause terrible damage. An eruption can blast hot lava, rock, choking gases and dust high into the air.

Thick layers of ash can bury fields and towns. Later, if it rains, the fallen ash can turn into fast-moving **mudflows**, smothering everything in their path.

▼ *When Mount Pinatubo in the Philippines erupted in 1995, mudflows buried the town of Bacalor.*

Lava flowing over the ground can cause forest fires, destroying wildlife for miles around. Eruptions can set off dangerous **landslides**, sending lumps of rock cascading on to roads and homes. Eruptions can also set off powerful tidal waves called **tsunamis**.

▼ *In 1980, Mount St Helens, USA, erupted, killing 61 people. Vast areas of forest were destroyed.*

Living with a volcano

Many people in the world live near volcanoes. They do not live in the most dangerous areas, such as near the crater. They live on the lower slopes, where it is easier to move to safety.

▼ Ash and lava threaten to destroy the village of Kapohoe, Hawaii.

Lava flows can destroy homes in villages or cities and kill people. Falling ash can bury whole towns. Landslides may cut off electricity and block roads.

If a volcano erupts unexpectedly, people who live nearby may have to be **evacuated**, or moved away, as quickly as possible.

▼ *These people in the Democratic Republic of Congo had to leave their homes when Nyiragongo volcano erupted in 2002.*

Useful volcanoes

Although eruptions can be deadly, many people are happy to live near volcanoes. Volcanic rocks and soils are rich in **minerals**. This makes the soil around volcanic areas perfect for growing crops.

▼ *Farmers grow rice and palms on the fertile volcanic soil in Bali, Indonesia.*

Some people believe the minerals in volcanic hot water and mud are good for their health. They bathe in the water to soothe their aches and pains. Hot volcanic mud is thought to be good for the skin.

▲ *These people in Vulcano, Italy, are taking a mud bath because they believe it will help to keep them healthy.*

Power from volcanoes

Rainwater soaks into the soil and seeps into the rocks below ground. In volcanic areas, magma under the ground heats up the water until it boils. This boiling water bubbles up through the rocks and shoots into the air as a natural fountain, called a **geyser**.

▼ Old Faithful, a geyser in Yellowstone National Park, USA, shoots up a fountain of water every 30–90 minutes.

This underground heat can be useful to people. Cold water is piped down to the hot rocks. The water heats up and turns into steam. The steam is piped up to a power station on the surface, where it is used to produce electricity and to heat homes.

▼ *Bathers in Iceland make the most of natural hot water, piped up from below the ground by the power station behind them.*

Volcanoes and change

Most volcanoes do not erupt all the time. Volcanoes that continue to erupt are called **active** volcanoes.

Dormant volcanoes are those that have not erupted for many years, but may still erupt in the future. Dormant volcanoes sometimes produce gases, but there is no lava or explosions in the crater.

▼ *Mount Fuji in Japan has not erupted for about 300 years.*

If a volcano has not had an eruption for thousands of years, it is called an **extinct** volcano. Over millions of years, extinct volcanoes gradually get worn away by the wind and the rain.

▼ *The Giant's Causeway in Northern Ireland was formed when a lava flow cooled very quickly. The volcano that caused it has long since disappeared.*

Predicting eruptions

Nothing can be done to prevent a volcano from erupting. But there are sometimes clues that can tell us when an eruption might be likely to happen. These clues help experts to predict some eruptions so that people can be moved to safety.

▼ *Scientists study Mount St Helens, USA, to find out when it is likely to erupt again.*

Magma and gases moving under volcanoes give off sounds and produce **vibrations**, or movements beneath the ground. Scientists measure the vibrations with special instruments. When the vibrations become bigger and more frequent, it is more likely that an eruption is going to happen.

▼ *Bulldozers in Italy dig barriers to prevent lava from Mount Etna from heading towards towns and villages.*

27

Volcano fact file

1. The oldest volcanic rocks on Earth are found in Greenland and Canada, and are about 4 billion years old.

2. The name 'volcano' comes from one of the Lipari Islands, Vulcano, which is in the Mediterranean Sea near Italy.

3. In 1902 Mont Pelée on Martinique erupted, killing 30,000 people in the town of St Pierre in less than a minute.

4. The Steamboat Geyser in Yellowstone National Park, USA, (below) shoots steam and water about 100 metres high. It is the tallest active geyser in the world.

5. In 1470 BC the gigantic eruption of Santorini, a volcanic island near Greece, caused a massive tidal wave and ash-fall, possibly wiping out a civilization on the nearby island of Crete.

6. The huge explosion of Krakatoa, Indonesia, in 1883 was the loudest eruption ever recorded. It was heard by people up to 4,700 km away. The eruption caused a tsunami 35 metres high that killed 36,000 people.

7. When Mount Pinatubo, in the Philippines, erupted in 1991, the ash cloud in the air spread round the world, blocking out some of the sun's rays. The temperatures in 1992 were much cooler than normal.

8. Parícutin, Mexico, was the first volcano ever to be observed from birth. After one day in 1943 the volcano was 50 metres high. After one year it had reached 336 metres high.

9 Scientists have found volcanic dust from eruptions that took place hundreds of years ago frozen in Greenland.

10 Kilauea in Hawaii, USA, has been erupting ever since 1983. New lava flows on top of lava that has cooled down, making the volcano grow.

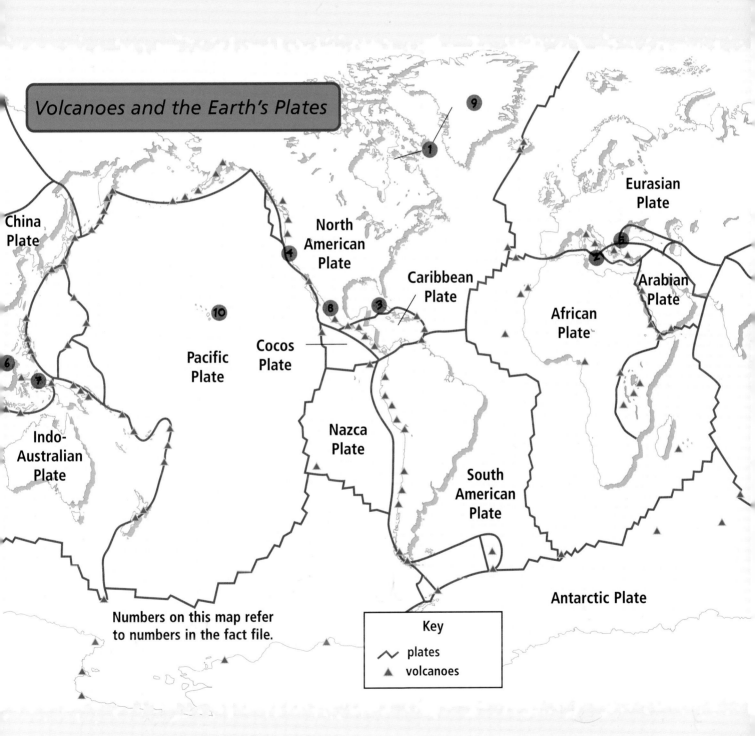

Volcanoes and the Earth's Plates

China Plate

North American Plate

Eurasian Plate

Caribbean Plate

African Plate

Arabian Plate

Pacific Plate

Cocos Plate

Indo- Australian Plate

Nazca Plate

South American Plate

Antarctic Plate

Numbers on this map refer to numbers in the fact file.

Key
~ plates
▲ volcanoes

Glossary

A a lava Thick, sticky lava.

Active A volcano that still has eruptions.

Chambers Large pockets of magma beneath volcanoes.

Cinder Lightweight volcanic rocks that have tiny air holes in them.

Core The centre of the Earth.

Crater A hole at the top of a volcano.

Crust The surface layer of the Earth.

Dormant A volcano that has not erupted for a long time.

Erupt When magma, gases and ash are forced to the surface of the Earth.

Evacuated Moved away to safety.

Extinct A word that describes a volcano that has not erupted for thousands of years.

Geyser A spring that blasts hot water and steam into the air.

Landslide When the slope of a volcano or hill collapses, or falls down.

Lava Magma that erupts on to the Earth's surface.

Magma Hot, molten rock that is found in the mantle.

Mantle The layer of hot, molten rock beneath the Earth's crust.

Mineral A chemical in water or soil that is good for plants and animals.

Molten Melted or liquid.

Mudflows When mud, made from ash and water, flows down a hillside.

Pa hoe hoe lava Runny lava. This type of lava forms shield volcanoes.

Plates Giant pieces of the Earth's crust that move around.

Pyroclastic flows Flows of hot gas, dust and rocks down the slopes of a volcano.

Shield volcanoes Big, wide volcanoes with gently sloping sides.

Tsunami A huge tidal wave caused by earthquakes or volcanic eruptions.

Vents Openings or 'pipes' inside a volcano, through which magma travels to reach the Earth's surface.

Vibrations Movements causing backwards and forwards shaking.

Further information

Books to Read:

Volcano (DK Eyewitness Guides) by Anita Ganeri (Dorling Kindersley, 1999)

Eruption: Story of Volcanoes by Anita Ganeri (Dorling Kindersley, 2001)

Mountains (Geography First) by Celia Tidmarsh (Hodder Wayland, 2004)

Our Moving Earth by Pam Robson (Watts, 2001)

Reading About: Volcanoes by Jen Green (Watts, 2003)

Violent Volcanoes (Horrible Geography) by Anita Ganeri (Scholastic, 1999)

Index

All the numbers in **bold** refer to photographs and illustrations as well as text.